Color Motivation

By Nakita Jackson

Acknowledgements

Once again, I want to thank my family and friends for your love and support, especially my three children, La'Kai, Tijai and Gabriella. My prayer is that I use my gift for the purpose it was given to me.

About this book:

My first book titled, Alphabet Motivation, used what we first learn in life (the alphabet) and alliteration to see motivation in the simplest things. This book uses color and acronyms to essentially do the same thing. If you learn to see the positive in everything, things we see every day will be reminders to stay motivated. Use the extra space at the bottom of each page to add your thoughts.

Enjoy!

RED - Rejoice Every Day

Red is the color of willpower.

Right now, you are being planted and the struggle has been with the old, hard soil. The ground is being broken up. That's what you are going through now - a BREAK UP. You need to break up/away from negative relationships, circumstances and mindsets. Once you're fully planted into the new soil, you will know that you can penetrate through the dirt and stones to get into a position to start blooming. IT'S A BREAK UP TODAY!!!!!!! Rejoice!

YELLOW - Your Expectancy Level Leans On Wisdom

Yellow is the color of energy.

Remember Rome wasn't built in a day - neither were you.

When you are near to giving up, just think about how far you have already come. Is it worth turning back? Is it worth giving up hope? Have you really tried your hardest? Maybe you see giving up as the 'easy option'.

Giving up isn't the easy option, in fact (in the long run) it's the hardest option. Imagine looking back in 5, 10 or 20 years, regretting all the things you didn't do and all the things you gave up on. Knowing that YOU stopped yourself from achieving your dreams, can be one of the most difficult things you will ever have to live with.

Make sure you live with no regrets. Keep going - it just takes time!

BLUE - Believe that Learning and Understanding Elevates

Blue is the color of wisdom.

Complacency is the enemy to your purpose. Where you are now is not where you are destined to be. Although you know that you are called to a higher level, you've accepted staying grounded.
Your emotional, mental and spiritual baggage that you are carrying is over the weight limit and instead of getting rid of the baggage, you would rather pay the penalty fee to keep it. You knew before you started on your way, that there is a limit to how much baggage you can carry.

When your baggage is too heavy, you cannot move through your process easily or quickly. You hold up others behind you on their journey. Now their destination is delayed because of your disobedience. Flights are being missed and delayed because of you.

Decide today to unpack those things that are not essential for your journey. Some of the stuff in your baggage needs to be destroyed. When you are not being promoted in the natural, look at what is holding you back in the spiritual realm.

GREEN - Get Ready to Evaluate Endless Needs

Green is the color of growth.

A tree is rooted where it's planted. Leaves grow and leaves fall. Fruit grows on some and fruit rots on some. That is what happens to us when we find good ground to be planted and sown into. Even if some of your family/friends/ideas fall off during one season, be confident that new people and ideas will blossom in another season. In the end, you're still standing!

PURPLE - Please Use Realistic and Purposeful Learning Examples

Purple is the color of royalty.

Let your transparency be your testimony. Sometimes you turn people away by pretending to be perfect all the time. Truth is, we've all messed up and had to ask for forgiveness.

When you are royalty, you own your mistakes and responsibility. You own what belongs to you both good and bad. Be your authentic self. Remember that your condition does not determine your position. Just like the prodigal son in the Bible, you can be eating with pigs and still be royalty.

BLACK - Being Loving And Caring is a Keepsake

Black is the color of power.

Have you ever had a day where everything seems to be going wrong? You feel like if one more bad thing happens, you may explode? Then you get to a place and someone says a kind word or does a kind gesture for you and it changes your whole mood. Remember that when you are out and you see others looking frustrated. One kind or loving word can change a person's day.

You have the power to shift the atmosphere for both yourself and others. Use your power daily.

BROWN - Breakthroughs Reflect Our Winning Nature.

Brown is the color of persistence.

Did you come across an obstacle? That's not a Stop sign, that's a Yield sign. You may need to yield to your doubt and look to merge with faith, then keep moving.

To those who have faltered on your dream: Stop letting people's opinions make you doubt YOUR vision and purpose. What one person thinks is a mess, may be beautiful to someone else. Always remember their vision is not yours. So, pick back up that pen and finish making your vision come to life. Your words create your reality.

ORANGE - Obviously Refuse Answering to Not Good Enough.

Orange is the color of freedom.

You can't move forward because of the chains binding you. They are keeping you from finishing your race. These chains hold you back from having great relationships. These chains have kept you from living your life to your fullest potential. If those chains were removed, you could follow your dreams. You see, you are refusing to acknowledge that you have the key to unlock those chains around you. You have yet to realize that no one has the power to limit your possibilities. You are more comfortable making excuses of why things won't work for you than you are in using the strength given to you by your ancestors.

Continue to live your life shackled by the chains you placed on yourself. Continue to get high off of your insecurities. Just don't sit in the way of those who have unlocked the chains that once held them back.

PINK - Pursue Instilling Needs of the Kingdom.

Pink is the color of hope.

There is always hope in every situation. If you can learn to change the way you look at things, you will have a more positive life. In singleness: Say you are being prepared for your spouse as they are being prepared for you. In marriage: say your marriage is blessed because your spouse has everything needed to be a complement to you and you have everything needed to be a complement to your spouse as well. In parenting: Say your child/children are great assets to society and they are blessings to their parents and the world. In sickness: Say you are healed and your body is coming into alignment with the way it's supposed to function. In employment: Say you're flourishing in a job that pays you to produce.

WHITE - Working Hard Indeed Takes Encouragement.

==White is the color of tenacity.==

Here's the scenario: You step into the ring and get knocked down on the first hit.
Victim mentality: I'm getting out of the ring because they are better than I am. I can't do this. They are strong and I am weak. I tried. I should have never gotten in the ring.
Champion mentality: I will not quit. That one punch did not knock me out of the ring, so I'm still in the fight. I will keep on fighting until I am better than my opponent.
LIVE YOUR LIFE AS A CHAMPION!!!!

GRAY - Garner Respect Amongst our Youth

Grey/Gray is the color of security.

Remember that when you are going through a storm in your life, you are never alone. You have silent cheerleaders watching and rooting for you to make it because people think, "If you can make it, so can I!"

or

GREY - Gleefully Remember to Encourage Yourself

Sometimes the hardest thing to do is to find strength to encourage yourself when you are the one going through a storm. Think about all the good things that happens after a storm: grass is greener, trees grow stronger, harvest grows, pollen is washed away, etc. Even though during the storm, it may get dark, you have to remember that the purpose of the rain is for growth.

GOLD - Go Out Learning Daily

Gold is the color of success.

Never think that you have learned all there is to know in life. Every day there is something new to be learned. Take time throughout your day to sit back and observe things. You can learn from people, animals, insects and objects. Most live their life in a hurry and miss opportunities for growth.

SILVER - Search Inward Looking for Value, Encouragement and Respect.

Silver is the color of fluidity.

We are all creative artists. No matter what the day brings, you paint the picture and write the story. You decide if it's a masterpiece or bestseller. Don't give anyone else the paintbrush or pen to your life's happiness.

Your life today is shaped by the words, thoughts, and actions you sowed yesterday. If you want your tomorrow to be different, change what you say, think, and do today.

VIOLET - Victory Is Overcoming Limits, Egos and Trials.

Violet is the color of victory.

Learn to gain strength from your struggles; power from your pain and faith from your failures.

For we wrestle not against flesh and blood.....The enemy is not afraid of your outer strength, but rather your inner strength. Use your sword (Word of God) instead of your hands. Declare today that you will not spend your time defending your purpose. You will instead speak what God has spoken to you as you continue to walk the path destined for you.

TEAL - Teach Examples And Lessons

Teal is the color of leadership.

I was thinking about the saying: "Throw me to the wolves and I'll come back leading the pack." Doesn't that make you a wolf too? So, they changed you and you became the toughest wolf? Be more like: "Throw me to the wolves and I'll have them thinking they are now sheep."

Reach within and establish the leader in you. Don't be so quick to always follow the crowd. What you have in you is great and should be used to show others the light in this sometimes-dark world.

BURGUNDY - Bring Understanding, Respect and Greatness to Undermine Neglecting to Develop Yourself.

Burgundy is the color of mental stamina.

Your life is in your hands, but you must learn to gain control of your thoughts. All your problems of fear, failure and doubts are because your MIND is ruling you… Take control of your mind and your thoughts. Every day, bit by bit, watch your thoughts.

No thought lives in your head rent free. Each thought you have will either be an investment or a cost. It will either move you toward happiness and success or away from it. It will either empower you or disempower you. That's why it is imperative you chose your thoughts and beliefs wisely each day.

BEIGE - Believe Everyday Is Going to be Excellent.

Beige is the color of progression.

Right now take a look down at your steps. Did you move forward at all today toward your goal or did you take a step backward? As they teach in football, if you have the ball in your hand and you're getting tackled, fall forward because you still made progress.

ROSE - Rely On Self Expression

Rose is the color of self-control.

Even if you rip a page out of a book, it doesn't mean those words were never there. Don't try to erase anything from your past because everything is lining up for the wondrous climax. Keep turning the pages and watch you go from victim to victor!!!

If you let the actions and words of others cause you to react outside of who you are, then you have handed them the steering wheel to your life. Don't relinquish your control.

CYAN - Clear Your Animosity Now.

Cyan is the color of reality.

During this season, take inventory of who you allow around you. Are the people around you Whiners or Miners? When you are faced with a test, do they complain that life is not fair or do they encourage you to find the gem inside of you?

You cannot put any energy into being frustrated with circumstances you have no control over. People will make promises to you and then back out. People will lie to you repeatedly. People will talk about you. People will not support you like you had hoped. Do not waste another minute being surprised or disappointed. It happens to everyone; even those who are winning.

MAGENTA - Make A Goal to Examine Negative Thoughts and Actions.

Magenta is the color of expectation.

I've seen people get excited when they hear about "Seed time and Harvest." They are in anticipation knowing that what they've sown is about to be harvested. They don't understand the concept fully though. They are only thinking of benefits, but they have forgotten that they have sown negative seeds and harmful words as well. Remember that what you sow will eventually be reaped. Example: If you say that what someone else is doing will not work, you are speaking death to their vision. Don't be surprised if what you decide to do does not work. Even if you don't believe in what others are doing, speak life to their dreams and visions.

TAUPE - Think About Understanding the Purpose in Everyday.

Taupe is the color of flexibility.

Latin proverb: Aeque pars ligni curvi ac recti valet igni. Translation: A piece of bent wood and a piece of straight wood are equally suitable for the fire. Meaning: It doesn't matter if everything is going good in your life or you're a mess right now, we all are put through the fire to fulfill a purpose.

PERIWINKLE - Purpose, Encouragement and Reassurance Is What Is Needed to Keep Life Exciting.

Periwinkle is the color of illumination.

The automobile industry upgraded vehicles and equipped them with automatic lights that stay on during the day as well as the night. You need to do the same as you travel through this life...keep your light shining in the day and night. Do not use the On and Off switch because you may forget to turn it on when you are going through storms and darkness.

FUCHSIA - Focus Unwaveringly on Challenges to Heal being Stuck In Adversity.

Fuchsia is the color of focus.

Focus on where you are going…not where you are right now. Speak life to your circumstances, situations and challenges. Create the vision of a brilliant future full of purpose. Adverse circumstances will try to hinder, discourage, shape and mold you, but stand firm; You will come through this even stronger and more powerful than before.

LIME - Love In Motion Everyday

Lime is the color of love in motion.

Have you ever noticed that when people who walk and speak or nod a greeting to others, often seem to have more pep in their step? They may smile at you and it becomes contagious. That's because love flows from the heart and the heart has a beat that we should all keep rhythm with. Love should not be only spoken, but rather shown as well. People need to see you love them not just hear it.

PEACH - Prepare to Enlighten And Change History.

Peach is the color of purpose.

If you're traveling, do you hold your baggage in your lap while you are on your journey? No, you store them in the trunk of your car or below in an airplane or bus. Now why are you trying to carry baggage with you on your life's journey? Those things need to be stored in the back (past) or beneath you (to step on to take you higher).

Every person who changed history, was once a child with dreams. During their youth, they took in what was said to them, done to them or what they had done. Finally, when it was time, they harvested that knowledge and made history.

There is nothing that happens to you that is wasted. Everything in your life serves a purpose. So, remember to be transparent when telling your testimony to others. You just might change history.

LAVENDER - Lend A Voice Encouraging New Dreams to Evoke Readiness.

Lavender is the color of movement.

Something powerful I was listening to a few years ago: People like to say they'll wait to do something as soon as they get their "ducks in a row." Think about this...when you see ducks just sitting are they in a row? No! When do you see ducks in a row? When they are moving. So, if you keep sitting there waiting to get your ducks in a row, you'll always be sitting. Your ducks will line up when you start moving toward something. Decide today that you will act on your dreams.

INDIGO - It's No Defeat In Going On.

Indigo is the color of endurance.

In this race called life, Yesterday ran its part and handed the baton over to Today. Now it's time for you to do something that will move you forward before Today passes the baton to Tomorrow. Think Positive, encourage yourself and others, get out and walk, go into that interview saying that position is yours, etc. Whatever you do, keep moving along. If you drop the baton; stay in your lane, pick it up and keep going.

MAIZE - Mentally Antagonizing Insecurities will Zap Energy.

Maize is the color of mental clarity.

We suffer more from imagination than from reality. What stops most is fear, not hurt.

The biggest fear most people have is looking foolish in front of others. If you can control this fear, you will be surprised by how many amazing things you can accomplish in your life when you're not worrying about what others think of you.

If you keep looking for a window of opportunity, you will only be on the inside looking out at others who walked out of the door of fear and into their purpose. Choose today to go from one who looks out the window to one who steps through the door.

Bonus Shades of color:

NEON - Never Engage in Obvious Negativity.

Neon is the color of positivity.

Never let others pull you into their negativity, but rather, raise them up into your positivity. Some people are assigned to you as a Judas to get you to your purpose, so accept that what is meant for evil is actually the nail needed for your cross.

PASTEL - Place A Special Task on Evoking Love.

Pastel is the color of motivation.

At the end of the day, no matter what you have endured, be encouraged to let your light shine. Love begets love and if you can stay motivated to love beyond what you are feeling, then you have been successful in fulfilling your purpose in the world.

About the Author

Nakita is an author, poet and motivational speaker. What began as simple Facebook posts used to motivate others, became the driving force that fueled her first book of many. She loves to use occurrences in life to show others that finding motivation daily is as simple as changing your thoughts. Nakita has a unique ability to make every obstacle a learning experience while explaining it in the simplest of ways.

Other books by Nakita Jackson:

Alphabet Motivation

Contact Information:

Website: www.nakitajackson.com
Email: Najackson14@yahoo.com

Made in the USA
Columbia, SC
06 October 2017